FOI

MW00879211

We often long for a loving, fulfilling, passionate relationship. When it finally comes, the joy we experience seems unquenchable. There are times, however, that this blissful experience takes sharp turns through the dark caves of deception, doubt, and frustration, and inside the deep crevices of pain and confusion.

It is then that we find ourselves reaching for the light and peace we once shared with that special person. We find ourselves searching for hope and understanding. We wonder whether our relationship will heal, and if we'll love again.

In this book the author takes you on a poetic journey over the undulating terrain of love. The poems carry you over the hills of pleasure and passion, dating and marriage, and guide you through the valleys of pain and confusion. Ultimately, you are shown the pathway to renewal and starting again...as love continues.

Table of Contents

Part 1: Pleasure and Passion

No. 1................................. Red Ink Pen

No. 2 ....I Never Felt

No. 3 ....Alarm Clock

No. 4 ....You Rock

No. 5......................Intercontinental Love

Part 2: Real Love

No. 6..Life

No. 7.............................Weekend Visit

No. 8 ....The Perfect Recliner

No. 9 ....The River's Delta

No. 10 ....First Comes Marriage

No. 11 ....The Overseer

No. 12 .....First Aid for Your Sprained Heart

Part 3: Pain and Confusion

No. 13 ....What Is It
No. 14 ....Confusion
No. 15 ....The Best She Ever Had
No. 16 ....Before Your Mask Was Gone
No. 17 ....Low, Slow, Funeral Song

Part 4: Love Renewed

No. 18 ....Met Him Online
No. 19 ....Today
No. 20 ....A Lovers Bath: Morning Water
No. 21 ....I'll Wear White
No. 22 ....Love

Part 1
Pleasure and Passion

RED INK PEN

This pen I write with drips red
The color of passion,
The color I see in my head.
As it moves across the page
Etching out feelings...of things not yet said.
This pen drips the color red.

I NEVER FELT

I never felt so much in my life,
The want to fly.

I never felt so much in my life,
This feeling...high.

I never felt so much in my life,
The desire to see.

I never felt so much in my life,
Distance...you from me.

I never felt so much in my life,
You, I'd miss.

I never felt
So much.

ALARM CLOCK

Can I be your alarm clock?
Tick-tock, tick-tock.

Early in the morning through your dreams I,
Flip-flop, flip-flop.

Mechanical? No.
Biological? It is.

Feel the beat in your head and begin to rise.

I'm not there, but just the thought of me,
Opens up your eyes.

YOU ROCK

Because of your sweet texts... You Rock
And you go the distance... You Rock
Flowers for no particular hour... You Rock
Your kisses, your hugs, your rubs... You Rock
Sexy from head, to Rock, to toes... You Rock
Kindness beyond measure... You Rock
In moments of pleasure... You Rock
Intelligence packaged... You Rock
I could keep at this... You so Rock
And just like that M.J. song I wanna rock with you.

INTERCONTINENTAL LOVE

I think of the ocean vast and wind.
I think of it touching earth with a crashing tide.
I think of the air filled with clouds.
I think of space between there and now.
I think of time 13 hours ahead.
I think of nights, you in my head.
I think of flying far away.
I think of the distance and know to pray.

I question the situation when I return.
I question your desires. Are they firm?
I question your peace. Is it there?
I question if in your mind, there is fear.

I know in my heart where I want to be.
I know the love between you and me.
I know about oceans vast and wide.
I know about earth and crashing tides.
I know about clouds filling the air.
I know there's only time between me and there.
I know of flying far away.
I know of flying back where I plan to stay.

Part 2
Real Love

LIFE

You think you understand it.
Yet still you question why.

You think that you can handle it.
But, still sometimes you cry.

Just when you think
You have it all figured out.
You're comfortable,
You're satisfied,
Decided to live without doubt.

You say, "I'll be happy just where I am."
I've tried this,
I've tried that,
And still can't work the plan.

Then all of a sudden something happens,
And the complacency is gone.

Never thought in my wildest dreams,
This friendship would be born.

But now it's here. What will we do?
Understand it?
Handle it?
Cry?
Ask why?

Or simply let it fly?

And enjoy this new friendship
Life has brought to you and I

WEEKEND VISIT

I checked the newspaper and the internet
And this is what's on my mind.
For us to do together
As we spend quality time.

Enjoy each other
Love the weather
Have fun and relax.

Communicate
Reflect on the past
Play, learn, and laugh.

These are the activities
That I could find.
And, would you believe
Not one costs a dime?

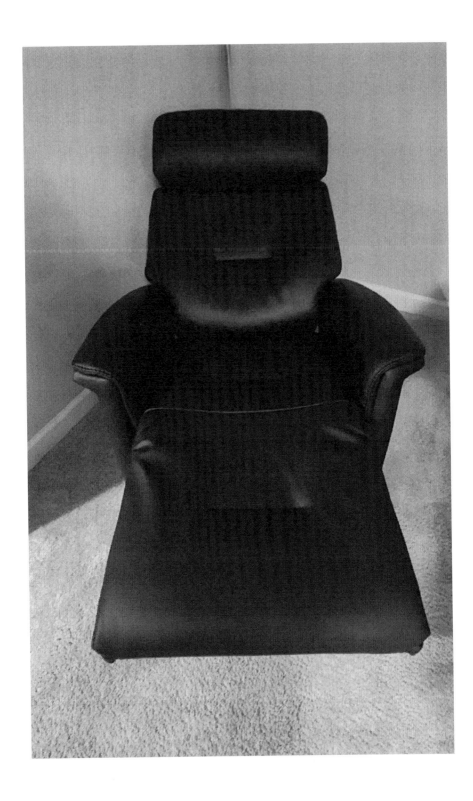

THE PERFECT RECLINER

It's been a long search for that perfect item
One I just have to find.

I've searched here. I've searched there.
But, I know I'll see it in time.

You see this item is special, a really dire need.
But, I can't just choose any one, this one must be for me.

The material...brown - sort of like leather. The arms...big and firm.
A place where I can stretch my legs, maybe a heater...my back to
warm.

See, I've worked for a long time, doing this all alone.
This perfect item, I need it when I come home.

To rest in those strong arms, the feel of leather against my skin.
To stretch my legs, lay back, and let warm thoughts soak in.

You see, I need a recliner, a fixture where I can be free.
This recliner will be the separation between stress and me.

After years of shopping for a recliner, one in which I can rest.
I'm glad I waited long enough, until I found the best.

THE RIVER'S DELTA

Wildly passing through the midst of earth
The two rivers flow
Turning, churning, carrying dirt
Their ends no one seems to know

Their paths run parallel
Passing the same scenes
But, their waters never touch
A meeting place not seen

The pattern of their waves
They look much the same
Some big and troublesome
Other's quiet and tame

What is it that connects these two rivers
Their origins far and wide
It is a place that is located
A little further down in time

A place where two rushing rivers
Join in a peaceful calm
It is at the delta in the river
Two rivers become one.

FIRST COMES MARRIAGE

Wow, I never expected my day to be quite like this
Sitting in the pastor's living room soon to kiss.

Not the ordinary kiss, but the kiss that unites
Your life unto mine, what was separate, twine.

No frills,
No fanfare,
Just family,
And a friend,

But, none of this matters
With you, my life I want to spend.

To honor my creator,
To keep his temple free from sin
There's no way this could be wrong
In obeying we will win.

THE OVERSEER

Overseer,
Overseer unconquerable,
His overseer's name was Life.

A whip
Used for whipping
For stripping of dignity, respect
Used for the causing of strife.

Breaking down what stood tall,
Belittling that which was great
The overseer who got his promotion by the turn of our countries fate.

He came into position subtly speaking the words, "Laid Off."
This overseer seemed reasonable, his words somewhat soft.

The sting of those words for a while he would not feel.
Until in the end, the effects were strangely real.

Hold up!
Who set up this here overseer?
Do his duties ever change?
When does he put away his whip?
Why must the spirit be tamed?

Come here Mr. Overseer.
Can I talk with you for a while?
That man you are whipping is the provider for me and my child.

Give him a chance to stand up!

A minute to breath in fresh air!
For he is a man, my man!
New words let him hear!

Words full of power, like "Yes, I have a job for you."
Do you hear me Mr. Overseer?
Will you please think this through?

Overseer?
Overseer, unconquerable?
Mr. Overseer?
Mr. Life.

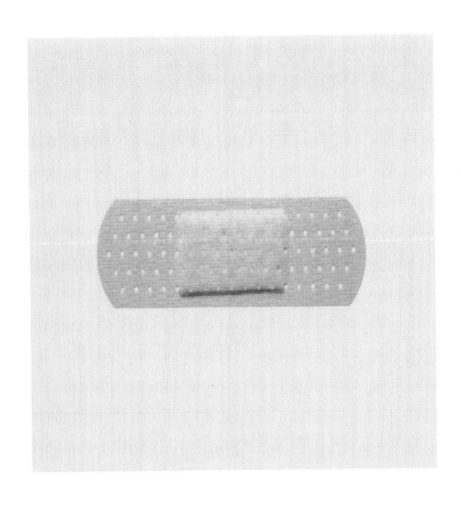

FIRST AID FOR YOUR SPRAINED HEART

Just because it wasn't broken,
Doesn't mean it should go without care.

So, with these words,
I hope to let you know I'm sincere.

I'm sorry.

I'll take the antiseptic lotion and wipe it clean.
I'll be a Band-Aid and stick you back to me.
Next, I'll use this special pad to remove the scar.
And I hope the next sprains, will be few and far.

I'm sorry.

I really don't like the feeling,
Knowing you're upset with me.

So, as I mend you,
I mend me.

Part 3
Pain and Confusion

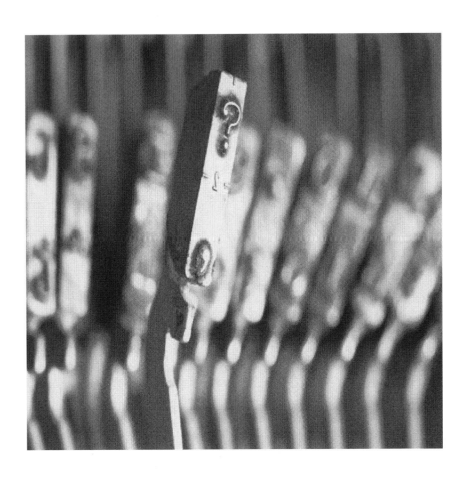

WHAT IS IT

What is it, when
You're confused by men;
Their honesty, your trust?

What is it, why
Love passes you by?
Your heart doesn't open to it.

What is it, how
You long for joy?
That joy only he can bring.

What is it, or who
Can change these things
Like the trepidation in your heart?

What is it, what
Do you truly long for?
A man, or just peace within?

The sooner you find the latter
The cycle will stop its spin.

CONFUSION

Enter a mind of confusion,
A mind that belongs to me.
A place of warfare,
A place where I'm not free.

A spiritual...a physical...a battle,
That's what's in my mind.
A place where I'm a prisoner,
Not freed by time.

Enter my waking moments,
Heart heavy and full of woe.
Help me release this confusion
My mind no longer can tow.

Enter my world, my spirit, my soul.
Enter emotions, deep.
Grab my hand and pull me.
Place in my hand the key.

Lead me through the darkness,
Take me to the line.
Where I cross over from confusion,
Into peace of mind.

THE BEST SHE EVER HAD

What have I turned into,
Some sort of Private-I?
Opening drawers, checking notebooks
Calling girlfriends from times gone by.

I never was the type of person
To go around and snoop.
All in search of a good reason
To give you the boot.

Why am I looking for more?
Have you not done enough?
Why is it so hard?
Why is it so rough?

It's almost like I don't know
If I'm looking for a reason to stay,
Or a reason to go.

Right now, I feel real stupid
Calling your ex-girlfriend.
She's like what's wrong with you?
He's the best boyfriend I ever had!

BEFORE YOUR MASK WAS GONE

Loving you was like loving sin
A false picture of peace waiting to do me in
I thought of you as a recliner
I called you my resting place
But now my minds all crazy
Spinning in space

I claimed you, said you would be mine
Forever, for a lifetime
That was before I knew you
Before I knew you'd lie
That was another place
A different time

You came telling me all the great things you were not
A producer, a scholar, a man who loved a lot
Yet all you could do was put me down
And discredit what I had
Everyday yelling, screaming, raging
Or, walking around looking sad

Yes, a cheat indeed
Because you've cheated me
Of my time, my freedom, my complete sanity

So now we're married and I'm stuck
That's just what you planned on
Had to hurry up and tie the knot
Before your mask was gone

LOW, SLOW, FUNERAL SONG

Lord, I need you to help me
I don't know how to make this work.
But every time I try and leave
You tell me, "Stay put."

We said divorce wasn't an option
But that was in the past.
I've got to get out of this relationship
And save my sanity fast.

Lord my life's playing like a sad movie
Not a smile all day long.
This ain't no marching tune
It's a low, slow funeral song.

One week I see a ray of hope
The next things fade to black.
Is it the spirit of forgiveness,
Or simply faith I lack?

I trusted you in the beginning
But maybe I was wrong.
Why would I claim in His son's name
A low, slow funeral song?

Year one my emotions took a beating.
Year two his sins were brought to light.
Year three I feel like I'm being lowered in a grave,
Piles of dirt shutting out the light.

Yes, I've reached the lowest of low

Talk about a relationship gone bad.
I really wish I could walk away,
But two kids I've already had.

Lord my life's playing like a sad movie
Not a smile all day long.
This ain't no marching tune.
It's a low, slow funeral song.

My relationship is dying,
But Lord Jesus! Let it die in you.
And at its resurrection,
I know you will renew.

A spirit of peace, a spirit of joy, a spirit of forgiveness
A spirit of love, a spirit of hope, a spirit of kindness
Longsuffering, meekness, a spirit of happiness

No funeral song
Just rejoicing all day long.

Part 4
Love Renewed

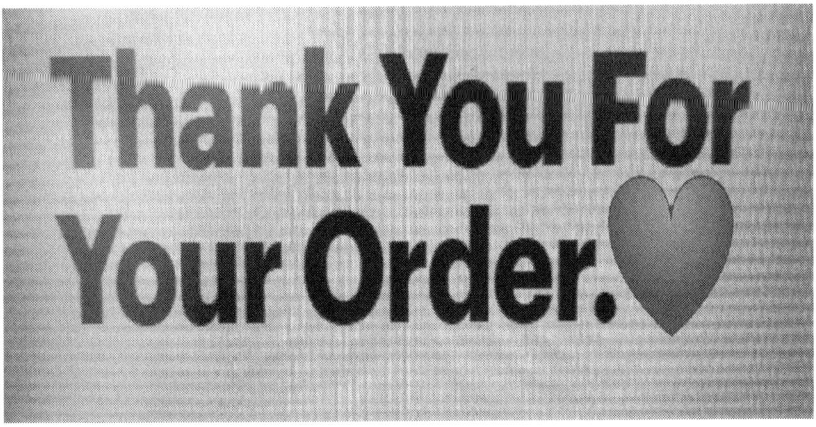
Thank You For
Your Order.

MET HIM ONLINE

Singly,
Individually,
You,
Me.

Sought out something.

A possibility,
A maybe,
A surety.

Surely, we
Could find...online?

In due time.
The question will become a comma,
Or a period.

Infinite?
Finite?

Something more?
Something less?
A quick mingle?
A hot tingle?

Another Christian single...
Hoping to leave singleness.

TODAY

Today,
May your day be filled with the same excitement that fills my spirit,
The same happiness that fills my heart,
And the same joy that fills my mind,
As I think of you.

A LOVERS BATH: MORNING WATER

Drip Drop, Drip Drop
Dripping, Dropping,
Flowing, Running,
Spreading, Rushing,
Cooling, Refreshing,
Calming, Wetting,
Water

I'LL WEAR WHITE

I'm wearing a white dress
And everyone is here.
This day is for us
For you and me my dear.

To show the world
Our love for one another
What God hath joined together
Let no man put asunder.

As I walk down the aisle
Your hand to join with mine

I have to think back to our beginning
I have to stop and smile.

Who could have seen this day
Who could read this unwritten page
Who could cause us to fall in love
Who, but He who sits above.

As the preacher pronounces us man and wife,
I know I'm glad that with you
I will spend my life.

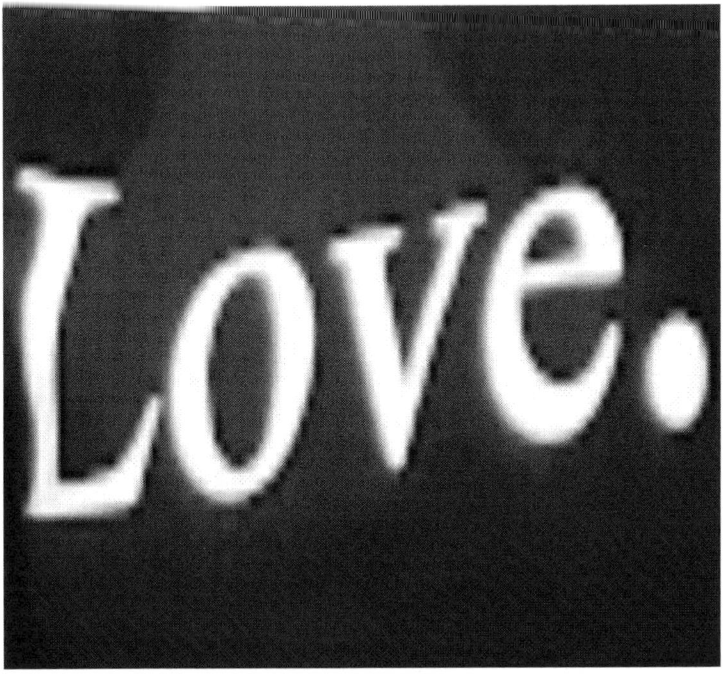
Love.

LOVE

Love
The beginning
The middle
The end.

Love
A feeling
A sound
A touch.

Love
To be felt
To be shared
To be expressed.

Love
To be continued...

Special Thanks to the Ones Who Loved, and Learned to Love, with Me and Apart from Me...

Made in the USA
Columbia, SC
30 October 2024

45269687R00035